The Immense Opportunities of Having Your Own Business

Acknowledgement

This is my first book ever. Perhaps it will be the first book of many, perhaps it will be the first book of few, who knows? Nevertheless, I appreciate you taking the time to read it. I would not have been able to write this book without the outstanding help, inspiration and love I get from my partner, Liza. Thank you for everything you give me, day in and day out.

This book is written with the sole purpose of looking at the benefits of starting and owning your own business, rather than being owned by someone else´s business. Sure, the decision of making the move onto something greater might be a hard choice filled with pros and cons, but I can promise you here and now, there will be more pros than cons.

 The reason you bought this book and chose to read it must be a sign that you are striving for more, something greater for either yourself or your family, or even both.

The idea itself is already an amazing move, but it is not enough just yet. We both know that there are tons of things which has to be figured out first, but in the end, you will be a whole new person filled with confidence and end up with a successful story, and perhaps pockets filled with whatever you want to fill them with.

The list of possibilities when having your own business is endless. One of the most popular ones is higher pay because you are the one who decides how much you can earn through hard work and dedication. Another one is more time with your family simply because owning a business in today´s world could offer different working hours than the classic 9am-5pm job. Which is great because no one likes to spend most of their life at work when they can do what they really love.

Just imagine. Being able to decide your own working days and have predictability. You know exactly what the next week brings, not because someone told you what to do, but because you, and only you made the decision about what to do and what to make money on. Think about this for a second.

It is your decision, and this is where an own business comes into play. Turn your passion into profit. Love what you do, and you will have no limits.

Think about why you want to start a business and the three things you want to accomplish with it. Some might do it for the money, or the fame, or the security for the family, but what is your reason? Is it money? Is it fame? Is it security for your family? Write it down, print it out or stick to the good old pen and paper and frame it. Frame it and hang it over your bed and remind you what you want.

To show you the importance of this, I will provide you with a step by step list on how to go forward with this.

1. Find your WHY. We will come back to this later on in this book with more details.
2. Write it down
3. Print it out
4. Frame it
5. Hang it where you can see it every day
6. Remind yourself of it every day when you look at it

Table of Contents

The immense opportunities of having your own business

"Success is not the key to happiness. Happiness is the key to success. If you love what you are doing, you will be successful."

- Albert Schweitzer

This book is being written on a Sunday afternoon to raise the awareness about all the opportunities an own and self-made business brings. The key, hereby, is to know that it doesn't have to be a massive international corporation with location all around the globe in order to be a great business. A business can be anything from a local construction business, online ad agency, local barber or an online shop for either drop shipped products or self-made products. Whatever it is, it can be yours if you want it to be, unless you enjoy a 9am – 5pm job, but since you are reading this book, I assume you are not. You want something more. Something bigger, something with a greater purpose than just making your boss a wealthy person.

I mean, I understand, and so do many other people, but not everyone. There will always be people who will try to make you stay in your job, who will try to kill your ideas and hopes. But trust me, as soon as you have gotten onto the thought of having your own business and being able to decide your own salary and working hours, your inner beast is on the way out. And remember, the power of your beast is only limited by you. As soon as it's free, clear way because it is about to take over.

Keep feeding it to realize the immense possibilities of having a self-owned business. Just imagine going to work and your name is on the door. Your employees, if you would have a business which requires employees, would greet you on the way in with the respect you deserve. You would have a coffee on your desk when you'd come in and your working day would start in an industry and sector which you love, because you chose to be there rather than somewhere else.

I chose to include "if you would have a business which requires employees", because with the possibilities the market offers today, there is not always a need for employees. In many cases you can handle it all by yourself, from your private computer on your couch at home. We will come back to some examples of businesses like this later on but let me give you a hint of what the reason behind these solutions are: Technology.

It's a beauty. It has changed this world in a way no one could imagine 20 years ago. I mean, who could have predicted in 1999 that the majority of people, unfortunately mainly in the Western world, has an average on two cars per household, flat screens and a phone in the pocket that is capable of handling every request.

This book is written just like that. As if the thoughts poured right out of my brain and into my hands. As if the information just came and got sent straight down to my fingers and onto the computer keyboard. The wording is chosen to make it a smooth ride, to make it float like a light boat on a river, and to make the reading less dull, more interesting and hopefully more entertaining.

Introduction to the rest of your life

"If you are not willing to risk the usual, you will have to settle for the ordinary."

-   Jim Rohn

There are many questions in life which have to be answered. What should you study? Does everyone know what they want to become when they grow up? Do I need good grades to get a job? How do I become successful? Do I have to get a low-positioned job and work my way up to become a boss one day? Can I have my own company? Do I need money to start a business? I mean, this is just a needle in the haystack when it comes to tricky questions of how things will turn out in the future, career-wise.

However, no one can really predict the future unless you're having some serious gifted skills. Back on topic, these questions will never really be answered because you will never really know how things would have turned out otherwise if you didn't do exactly what you did. If you got rich by having an engineering degree, would you also have become rich if you started your own business early on, without that degree?

Not necessarily, but possibly, and if pursued correctly, most likely. You know why? Because you are your own boss, and this is key to determine your own success. And the best part is that it´s so very possible in today´s market.

We no longer live in a world where you grow up, enter the same line of business your parents were in by taking a job at the local factory and working a constant 9am-5pm workday. This is not our future and this workday is what is out of business. On the other hand, you might think "well, if that is out of business, then what is now in business rather than these classically hated 9am-5pm days?".

Well, my dear reader, I will tell you what is in business these days. Not related to anything but business because that is why I sat down to write this booklet.

What is in today is starting something for yourself. Read that sentence, "starting something for yourself". Imagine, you enter a massive journey of controlling your own business, your own working day, your own tools, your own partners, your own customers and so on. The list never ends and brings major possibilities which can happen when you decide on it.

Just think about it, you quit your 9am-5pm job which you have hated for the last _____ years and you are about to release your inner business beast which you know and can feel it´s waiting to be finally unleashed. You´re about to open the door to a brand-new life for you and your family. Just imagine it once again. Get used to imagining because that's key to a bigger meaning in life and new possibilities.

You won't get anywhere without imagination as well as the obvious and famous word, "GOALS". Sure, these doors also include some serious hard work, difficult choices and a rough path. It's not a play in the park. It's serious business, a business you are responsible for. But it will be a fun ride, because remember, you do what you love. I believe that responsibility is great. You make choices, you call the shots, ultimately it makes you grow and when something is yours, you make sure to keep it safe and you think things through.

However, the cool part about this is that the difficult choices does not affect your family and the valuable things in life in the same way as a depressing 9am-5pm job does. These regular jobs don't bring real happiness to anyone, nor do they bring in money, success or if you'd like, fame either. So, is it good having a regular job? The answer is; it depends. Well, of course it could be, for some people. Many people love having it because many companies are great with their employees & provide security, and we all know that. But that is not the topic of this book. We are not here to focus on the companies which are good with their employees or the ones having a great working culture.

We are here to make you take the step and make you realize what you can do, and maybe one day, hire your own employees and create a great working environment.

As with everything else, it depends. If you are a person who loves 9am-5pm jobs, great, that's just great for you. However, if you love those jobs, why would you pick up this book? Because I am not here to give compliments to 9am-5pm jobs, because I believe in the greater cause of immense opportunities, and those are not coming unless you start for yourself.

There's probably a part of you thinking "how the hell can I start for myself when I have no money to spare" or the classic "I don't know where to begin". My friend, that's why we have YouTube and Google to our expense. These tools, sources, playgrounds or whatever else you might want to call it, are the keys to everything in the life of business.

There are millions of people having the same questions as you do every day, and there are millions of others who had the question, figured it out and shared it with the rest. Either through articles, videos, blog posts, social media or some other shareable sources. Later on in this book, we will discuss why these tools are as great as they are, and why they are so helpful especially when starting for yourself. But then again, why should you listen to a 24-year old guy telling you about opportunities to start for yourself?

I highly believe in listening, not judging others but rather respecting them and their opinions. Everyone has a story and something to add to the table, and no one is empty handed. I believe everyone has a secret weapon they have built up and developed over time, if this secret weapon is knowledge of how to start a business, do math, sell a product or whatever it might be, no one is empty handed.

The Gods of Inspiration

"All progress takes place outside the comfort zone."

- Michael John Bobak

An important asset to the industry of business is "motivation" and people motivating others to believe. To believe they can do things they would have never thought they could. I am about to introduce you to three Gods of inspiration which will change your life.

The ones to come are not necessarily publicly declared as Gods of inspiration, and they might not be a role model for everyone. Everyone has their own role model and their own person they look up to. This is why, I would highly recommend you to find your own God within your desired field. Take their actions and inspiration and/or look at their stories and speeches for guidance when needed.

These "normal" guys are not only amazing speakers, but they have backgrounds and histories just like everyone else.

They wanted more, they made the decision to take the leap and with that have helped thousands, and in some cases, millions of others. Imagine going to bed knowing you helped millions of people. I can´t believe that anything could possibly beat this feeling.

These are my God of inspiration:

First person out is Grant Cardone. I have read his books and listened to his audibles and I am a huge, huge fan. The way he talks to you, how he inspires you is just spectacular. I only listened to him for five minutes and knew I "want this", I just wanted to drop everything I had in my hands and start a new business. He is a bestselling author, world´s #1 sales trainer, renowned speaker, international social media influencer and real estate mogul.

This guy is not messing around. But it wasn't always like this, and this is what makes him incredibly interesting. I don´t want to spoil his history to you, so just Google him and grab every piece of inspiration there is, purchase his books and listen to his audibles, because he will change your life.

Second person out is Anthony Jay Robbins aka Tony Robbins. He is an American author, philanthropist and a life coach. He changed my view of reading books early on because one of the first books I read was his famous "MONEY, Master the game". A massive book filled with knowledge from the very beginning all the way until the last word in the book. I couldn´t stop reading it because it was just too good to be put down. I would recommend every book he has ever published because of multiple things, however the main reason how he writes and how is strives to help others. He gets to the point every single time. He delivers, every single time. I am saying this as a fan to my fellow business seekers, and I recommend reading his books.

Third person out is Oprah Winfrey. You all probably know her from "The Oprah Winfrey Show", but she is so much more than that. In addition to be an American media executive, she is also an actress, talk show host, television producer and philanthropist. She grew up in poverty but changed her life upside down and now has a net worth of $2.7 billion. She took the hard choices and she succeeded like few else. She is a person filled with inspiration and knowledge. I strongly believe, everyone should look into her, read about her and her books, grab all the inspiration and knowledge possible, and never look back, because they will change you.

These three people are all well-known, and they have good reason to be. Personally, these are some of the people I read about the most, not only to get inspiration and insights, but to also remind myself that immense success is possible but does not come over night.

"Be thankful for what you have; you'll end up having more. If you concentrate on what you don't have, you will never, ever have enough."

- Oprah Winfrey

I constantly find inspiration in other people, if it is through real life conversations of people, through social media such as Instagram or Facebook, or if it is through books and audibles. I think social media is a great source to knowledge, inspiration and market updates. Depending on how you use them, social media can also be a great source of inspiration, so make sure to follow some Gods like the ones I mentioned before.

Personally, I follow everything from motivational speakers like the ones we just talked about, successful people such as Bill Gates and Jeff Bezos, financial markets which updates me on changes and market happenings. I feel like this gives me value and inspiration on a daily basis which is important to stay motivated and hungry.

These people are just some out of many who are constantly feeding your inner beast with power, strength and bravery. Hard decisions take bravery to come through on, and by listening to people like Grant Cardone, you constantly feed yourself with inspiration, you constantly feed your inner self with valuable nutrition helping you make the toughest decisions.

These are the times when motivational speakers or role models come into play. They can make a real difference in tough situations.

It is not always enough to listen to yourself and find inspiration and motivation from within. That's why I often, very often take to other people's words and inspirational stories to make myself walk that extra mile and handle the other client. Be confident enough in yourself to be able to ask others for either help or inspiration, or even tips and ideas.

Listen, Then Speak

"I owe my success to having listened respectfully to the very best advice, & then going away and doing the exact same"
-    G. K. Chesterton

The heading for this chapter is chosen because of the truth shared in these three words, and also because listening is a sign of respect for others. Fun fact; we would never have had the world we are living in today if it wasn´t for respect. We would still be stuck in year 1600 where wars, racism and constant issues were ruling the daily life.

And I mean, who wants to life in such a world. As I mentioned previously, this book is a straight up business book, or even a motivational book for people who wants greater things in life than making others rich.

Because I mean, why would you make other rich when you can make yourself rich. And when I say rich, I don't necessarily mean just in regard to money, also known as the bill-payers.

I also refer to time, freedom, low hanging shoulders and a happily family. What matters is your own definition of it. Just think about it, you can control your own working hours, you can choose when you want to work and when you want to be with your family, how much money you can earn and when you want to do what.

Of course, this is amazing, but it is also, for now, a theoretical aspect of what can be your life. In theory, everything is possible, but this example of having freedom, the feeling of being constantly revealed and knowing that you are able to support your family, is not just theory. That's the crazy part.

It's all possible with dedicated belief and positivity, and a spirit that never, ever quits. We will come back to the necessary tools you need to succeed, potential ideas and much more in just about a couple of pages, but first, it's time to imagine.

You are working the classic 9am-5pm job, your boss, who you are making rich by the way, is telling you to do a job which you hate. Either if it is to meet a disrespectful client and take orders from him or her, or if it is to read through thousands of papers to find this one sentence your boss just loves for some weird reason. No matter why, you're still doing it because you think that this is your purpose, maximum performance level and the only way to get through life. But let me tell you my friend, it is not. It really isn't. But instead of going back to work a 9am-5pm job, you decided to quit.

Instead, you are headed to your office, either if you choose to have an own space for it or if your office is at home. You know what you will do today because you are deciding it. You sit down in front of the desk and begin to work. You help client after client and bills them for the amount you feel is competitive and fair, and certainly the amount you deserve. Imagine then, the money goes straight into your bank account, not someone else's. Not to be egoistic, but one of the perks to have you own business is that you can pay yourself first. Be the first in line to receive the money you deserve. The money you have taken all the risk to receive.

You love your job because you chose to go this way. Your kids are coming home, and you can spend time with them, cook and be a proper role model with a happy smile planted on your face. This is what could be your day. The best part is that it can be even cooler, depending on what you prefer and picture for yourself. I am not going to decide on how it might look like because I can't.

You might think now that having your own business will only result in gold and green woods, but it will require hard work. You were up late working last night? Well, you still got to get up early in the morning, brew that coffee and get back to work. Because you still have to supply your clients with your services you have promised them. The more you dedicate your time; the more doors are opening. Doors full of opportunities and endless possibilities.

But you may wonder why I called this chapter "listen, then speak"?

That's a valid question. I chose to call it that way because when you think about it, can you even speak unless you have listened? Yes, some may say, but really, though?

Although being mysterious and mystical might be entertaining, I won´t hide the meaning of the sentences, and I will go straight to business. Because in this world, time is money. The meaning is the importance of reading and listening. Listening to massively successful people by both physically listening through their podcasts, videos and audibles. But also make sure to read their tips, stories and ideas and take inspiration from their successful journey and lay out on your own when you feel ready. "When am I ready" you might think. You never know before you try.

Reading is full of power. It´s free knowledge and printed tips. It literarily printed ways of how to become successful. We all know Bill Gates, right? He reads one book a week. Why? To always stay up to date, get new inspiration and to always grow, or maybe he just does it because he likes to read. No matter the reason, he is one of the most successful people of our time and has been the richest person in the world for years.

Reading gives you so much. Sure, every book cost, and if you read 52 books a year like he does, you will spend a lot of money of books. However, it is important to understand the value of reading. You invest in yourself for every word that you read. You grow for every page you cover, and the inspiration is massive, just massive.

I use the word "massive" a lot in my life because that is the common word that fits the most when it comes to the opportunities of starting for yourself. But let´s take a last moment to discuss reading. Although it is not the topic of this book and will not be brought up much more after this, but seriously, books, they are mostly written by people who have achieved something bigger and they have made the decisions of doing something greater.

Books by successful people are basically knowledge from the top shelf printed onto a small piece of paper feeding your brain with a knowledge you won´t get anywhere else for a couple of bucks. I mean, how amazing is that, huh? I didn´t always read a lot and when I first did, I became this new person craving for something better and bigger. I wanted to see new opportunities and seize them as hard and fast as I could.

Because, in the end, who doesn't want to have an own business and more control? This is where hard decisions and bravery comes into play, and it is what distinguished employee's from employers. Think about that for a second. Do you want to be an employee, or an employer?

Who Is Writing This and Why Should You Listen?

"People who succeed have momentum. The more they succeed, the more they want to succeed, and the more they find a way to succeed. Similarly, when someone is failing, the tendency is to get on a downward spiral that can even become a self-fulfilling prophecy."

- Tony Robbins

First, I want to bring attention to Tony Robbins again, if you haven't already heard of him, take a moment and Google him. He is one of my favorite mentors in the world of business. If you don't think you can start a business and have $100 000 dollars in sales in five years, he will not only change your mind, he will make you believe that you can have $1 million dollar in sales in five years.

I have read most of his books and when he releases a new one, I buy it immediately. His words are pure gold. Gold you can buy for $30 dollars. Make sure to check him out!

Second, you might wonder about the author of this book, how legit he is and why his words could possibly add value to your life. Well, I am putting together this book as a first big passion project because I have been where all of you have been.

Should I start something for myself or should I continue working an average job anyone else could do? That was the question running through my mind. But after reading tens of books, after listening to successful people and getting the inspiration I needed, I released the inner beast and it took over. I know what my future is, and my name is all over it because I am owning it.

I started my first business when I was 22 years old and it was a drop shipping store, I built on $30 dollars in start-up costs.

I put together ideas of what I should dropship. Everything from jewelry, fitness clothing, nutrition supplements, clothing and books came up, but I landed on fitness clothing. I mean, the industry is huge and is only headed one way, which is straight up. When it comes to having an online store, Shopify is gold. Pure gold, I´m telling you. They offer great services, tons of tools and important factors such as good payments options, themes, websites etc.

I chose drop shipping because it allowed me to have an online business, work from home which saves you costs of renting an office and office equipment, and no need for employees in the beginning because after building everything up, the administrative part is manageable by one person.

However, I strongly believe in constructive feedback, and during this period I had a person who looked at my work, my design and my layout. She gave me feedback and we discussed back and forth to achieve the best approach with the customers need in mind. In the end, it's your call, but when you spend so much time building a project, you might fall off topic from time to time. Therefore, by getting a clear mind from partner, could help you get back on track.

A drop shipping store does not require any storage costs either, unless you produce home-made products and you ship them. But since I wanted to avoid storage costs, I sold products for AliExpress which is the Chinese version of Amazon.

It offers tons and tons of products to great prices included shipping, and it lets you set your own prices. I put together Shopify and AliExpress and offered customers low-priced products included shipping, I set a price of 30% higher than retail-price and have a smaller cut and rather focus on volume. After all, there's two ways to do business, either based on volume, or price. But then again, it is not up to me to tell you how to run your business, my job is just to make you realize the benefits of having your name on the wall rather than someone else's.

Additionally, I started a website business, Adshoi.com, with my partner when we were both 24 years old, while she also started her coaching business Lizadulting.com, actually we just started both of them and customers are beginning to pour in. In other words, I´ve started two business before I am 24 years old with just two tools. Books as inspiration and my computer as execution. That's the beauty of today´s world, you can do so much with just a computer, thanks to the internet.

Having a partner can be great, it all depends on how you work together and what both parts are bringing to the table. In my case, we fulfilled each other's skills perfectly. She had a skillset which fulfilled my weakest areas. Design. But keep in mind, you do not need a partner to start anything. You and your inner beast is all you need, just make sure to keep feeding it.

So, what can you take from this small chapter? Well, the importance of reading cannot be put into words properly, and it is a key factor of inspiration and feeding the inner beast. Because although it is released, it still needs to eat. And the food it eats comes either through the form of books, motivational videos or speakers, inspiration through various sources and/or self-belief. It can come from wherever you decide, and it is up to you how you receive it and how you channel it.

Always believe in yourself, no matter what others can say, because they are often the ones who hold you back unless they are pushing you. But why would they want to hold you back?

Because they are comfortable with the current situation, and they are okay with living paycheck to paycheck as long as they can hang out with you and talk about the usual stuff about how life is and blame others or something along these lines.
But that's the thing, negativity kills, and you got to avoid it.
This is where goals come in.

A part of the chapter is "why should I listen"? Well, to answer that question, you don't have to. But since you are taking part of your valuable time to read this book, you obviously want someone to tell you what to do, or to get the inspiration necessary to make a decision of doing something else.

Or maybe the reason is a whole other story, so it is up to you if you want to listen or not, and I won't tell you what to do. But my story adds up to many others. I wanted to start something for myself, and I did. Now people want my services and I give it to them. I set my own prices depending on the project and I set my own working hours. In this way, I have a lot of more time with the people I love. So, listen to me or not, but I made the decision of doing something bigger, can you?

What Do You Need To Start and Succeed?

"If you look really closely, every overnight successes took a long time"

- Steve Jobs

Before I begin writing this chapter, I want to put in perspective the possibilities which are laying in front of you by starting for yourself. Just think about it and answer this out loud for yourself: "Should you make others rich or yourself rich?"

The importance of reading books like this and listen to audibles is that you read and hear what you desire and want to hear. This feeds you with powerful inspiration. For example, when you work a classic 9am-5pm job you are dedicating your time to a small paycheck for yourself, and a huge one for your boss.

A boss that is not smarter than you, not better, not anything. He or she in an equal but has taken choices resulting in where they are today. "I want to make myself rich, I want to give myself freedom, I want to give myself more time and I want to give myself what my family and I deserve."

Read it out loud and never forget these words. Say them every time you wake up and every time you go to bed. Tell them to yourself, your partner, your parents and share the thoughts to make them come alive. Because what good is it, if you don't believe in the words, and if you don't make it come to life? You have to take the words, make them stick to your brain, your heart and your inner motivation, and be proud of it.

The table on the next page is a famous tool when it comes to decision making. Write down all the pros and cons which comes to mind. Don't leave anything out to be able to make a good decision.

The topic now is: **"why should you start for yourself rather than working a 9am-5pm job?"**

Start for myself	**Work 9-5pm job**
Decide my own work hours	Relatively
Decide my own limits	stable
Pay myself first	monthly
Decide my own future	income
Have MY name on the wall	
Have unlimited possibilities	
Decide my business strategy	
Give myself what you deserve	
Be my own boss	

As shown above, there are so many more benefits of starting for yourself. Of course, it is not such an easy choice as I am putting it into words for now but see what it gives you. It's not just a different job, it's a different life. This is not even the whole list, and it's far from it. You can put down whatever you want here, and I want you to make your own drawing like this and fill it out.

Start for myself	Work 9am-5pm job

Write down what you think of the topic; **why should you start for yourself rather than working a 9am-5pm job?**

Because if you want something bigger and better, you got to see the benefits of having it and you got to imagine all the possibilities. But you also have to be aware of the potential outcomes.

As written in the drawing, the only "positive" side of having a 9am-5pm job is that you receive a relatively stable monthly income. For some people the pros and cons will vary depending on their preferences and personalities. Some people might prefer having a 9am-5pm job because there a million of great jobs out there, and these jobs are necessary to be filled in order to keep the society running. However, they do not fit for all.

I include "relatively" because when you work for others, you are never safe. You cannot decide your own future and you sure as hell can't decide your own working hours or salary. Draw a drawing like the one above, write down your thoughts and rethink your current situation. What can you do about it, what can you change and what are you going to do?

What can you/are you:

change	do about it	going to do?

How to run a business will depend on the business, your goals and strategies, but you will find the answer by putting off the time to find them. This is where beautiful inventions such as YouTube, Google, social medias and technology comes in.

There's no answer you can't find through one of these tools. As an example, let's say your dream is to write a book, what do you need to do that? Easy, you only need three things:

1. A computer or a pen and paper, depends on your preferences.
2. A place where you can write, and which fills your brain and body with inspiration, ideas and words.
3. Coffee, and lots of it. It's just how it is.

What if you want to have an online store to sell a homemade product which you know in and out and have been in the family for generations, work from home and spend more time with your family?

You need your computer and some time because you have to build the store either through Shopify which I recommend, through Wordpress or one of the other providers out there. There are hundreds of possibilities, where all of them are quite similar. However, not everyone knows how to build a website, and that's where YouTube comes in. Put off some time to watch videos and play around with the chosen provider and build something you like which puts your product in the spotlight. However, if you are not comfortable of building your own website, and would prefer to outsource this job, this is of course possible. There are tons of website builders out there to can put up a website in no time for a reasonable amount of money.

What if you want to start any other type of business? Well, there is no one-size-fits-all kind of approach to a question like this, but the positive thing is that your answers are available on either Google or YouTube. Use these inventions for what they are worth, because they will solve your problem, almost no matter what the issue is.

When I first started building my very first website, I found articles on google, guides on YouTube and valuable videos which solved my exact issues. I even posted questions on online forums where people answered my requests within a day. The internet is everything you need to start whatever you dream of. Use it for what it´s are worth, because it´s are free and constantly available, so never ever say you can´t figure something out, because the answer is always out there. You just got to find it.

Additionally, a tool which is an absolute game changer is the online learning platform "Udemy". Udemy is a platform full of professional learning courses where you will find everything you are looking for, and plenty of them. If you want to become an investment banker, they have multiple courses for you full of detailed videos and other materials.

If you want to become a developer, they have both frontend and backend options as well as tons of other ones. You might think "what should I do with just another course?" But that's the crazy part, most of the courses provide you with a certificate. In other words, you could become a proven professional within a specific field through the course. How wild is that?

But that's not the wildest part! You probably think these courses are going to cost you all your money and even a little more than that, but every now and then, Udemy have these massive sales periods. 90% discount is the standard of these periods which I have happened to notice, happens around every third month and it lasts for a couple of weeks usually.

In other words, I would not recommend you to go on some kind of shopping spree outside of these discounts' periods. Find your favorite courses, wait for the right moment and hit them hard when the time comes.

Professional courses which in many cases give you a certificate, for the net amount of $9.99. Just imagine, you can become a certified expert within your favorite field by spending some time watching videos, taking notes and reading through resources.

You can change your life with $9.99 and two days.

What Can I Do, I Need Ideas!

"The only limit to our realization of tomorrow will be our doubts of today."
- Franklin D. Roosevelt

If you have gotten to a point where you know that you want to start something for yourself because you know the benefits of doing it. You feel so damn ready, but you are not sure what to do? Then take two seconds to prepare, because I am about to give you some ideas which are proven to work.

Keep in mind, that more or less any idea, could theoretically work, it just depends on how it's approached and pursued. Did the idea receive the attention, time and dedication it deserved?

Be aware, there is no "work hard Monday to get rich Tuesday". You must realize that having your own business will result in hard work, ups and downs and some long days. This mostly affects the beginning of the process. Once you have established the fundamentals, you can run it with more predictability, and you will know what happens the coming week. Plan they how you like them. Be aware, although it might lead to some long days, you will still be able to achieve your defined success by having your own business. Even if your success is more time with the family. It will provide you will more flexibility and ability to work from home. Also, over time, while you develop and build your business, you get better and better at it. You get more insights, more knowledge and more strength to continuously grow and improve.

The era of technology is an absolute game changer and should be adapted by anyone who wants and can. It offers immense opportunities for thousands of different purposes, but mainly, in this case, opening new businesses. Before its time, it was never possible to open an online store, send emails, be on social media and so much more. While now, these technological inventions are now the fundamentals of millions of businesses. The technology came, it stayed, and it has been conquering since day one, and is not about to stop.

Take inspiration from technology and be the human form of technology to your greatest extent. There are many ways to interpret this sentence, but what I mean is that technology always develops, grows and improves. Do that same. Learn something new every day which makes you grow. But also, adapt it and use it for what it's worth, because we are talking about some serious amount and possibilities.

First potential business idea is coming up: you can start a drop shipping store. Because it gives you training on building a website, setting shipping rates and prices, choose products as so much more. But mainly, it shows you what the technology is capable of. I mean, you can start a business for $30 as a start-up cost and then $19 a month by using Shopify. Install the Chrome Extension "AliExpress" and sell products which you don't even own or take up any of your space. How it works; you showcase products owned by AliExpress, Amazon, Walmart or other stores through AliExpress. When a customer buys a product, you receive an order at the price you set. You fulfill the order by purchasing the product through AliExpress at retail price, the shipping information will be automatically filled out and you just have to press "send".

In other words, you sell at your own price, and buy at retail price. Shipping will obviously depend on the supplier. A drop shipping store is only limited by yourself and you can reach millions of dollars in sales a year. You can also create something yourself and sell it online through your own store. Although, this would require storage, but in the end, it all depends on your preferences, because it´s your business.

Second potential business idea: You could start an online advertisement agency by focusing on Facebook ads, Instagram ads or ads for other online platforms. Companies all over the world are using ads every single day to either find customers, business partners and so on, whereof many of them are looking for a cheaper provider. You can be this exact provider they are looking for. Ads are not about to run out since the internet and technology is taking more and more over, which means, your job would be future proof.

Just think about all the advertisements you see around you every day. This can be your main skill, your expertise and your future job. You could potentially own this market and be that someone who everyone comes to for tips. Dedicate yourself to use available tools such as YouTube and Google to become a master in this industry, build up a client list and charge them for your services. Putting up an ad could take as little as 5 minutes if you are an expert but could take days for someone who doesn't know it at all. Sell them your expertise at a price you choose.

More business ideas that use the incredible advantage of the legendary internet and all it's available tools and devices are:

Graphic designer	Website developer
Meal planning	Tour Guide
Translator	Blogger/vlogger
App developer	Social media consultant
Digital Marketer	Build Chatbots
Front end/back end developer	UX research
Copywriting	UX / UI design
Event planning	Travel planning
Interior design	Bicycle repair
Social media influencer	Clothing designer

There are hundreds of possibilities out there. The list above is just a very basic list of options reaching from technology inspired to the good old bicycle repairing business. One idea is not necessarily better than the other, it all depends how it's pursued. In my opinion, almost any idea can make you rich, successful, comfortable you name it, but it's all up to you and how you pursue it. Additionally, many of the ideas above are free to start up, and you can learn all of the necessary skills for it online. Either on YouTube, Google or social media accounts can you easily gather knowledge and inspiration. Use what fits you best, if it´s videos, informative articles or other materials. The point is, the information is out there and available for you, so you just got to grab it.

Another tip which gave me a lot of inspiration and ideas is the social media platform, Instagram. It didn´t give me direct ideas which I pursued on, but it made my brain think hard. Real hard. It made me more creative and it constantly ran in my mind like "what can I do", "what can I start" etc. By following business profiles like the ones that inspire you, you can use a social media platform for something much greater than just for fun.

You can become inspired, driven, motivated, smarter and it can make you grow in the fields you choose. There are thousands of brilliant profiles out there providing their followers with top-notch content.

Right now, to make this one step more real and in a new direction, pick up your phone or computer and whatever technology device you got next to you. As long as it can access social media, it´s good to go. Follow profiles like "World economic forum", "Grant Cardone", "Bill Gates", "Elon Musk" etc., and let the information inspire, motivate you and strive for greater things. If you love business quotes, follow someone who provides daily content of the best quotes.

World economic forum constantly provides you with detailed videos of the current situation of the world with both business-related content as well as environmental content. They even include weekly "tests" and tons of fun facts. While, for example, the others provide you with constant reminders of what is important in business, their stories and/or their current projects. This will for sure keep you going, keep you motivated, and it will want you to reach new heights. Every single day. This is the power of social media and provided content from successful people.

Turn Your Passion Into Profit

"Stop chasing the money and start chasing the passion."

\-   Tony Hsieh

Everyone has a passion. A passion can be sports, writing, reading, helping others, learning a new skill, a certain line of work etc. Whatever it is, you can use it for something bigger.

If you have a passion for writing, you can either work for a newspaper or a local magazine, or you can skip that, dedicate you time to write your own books or biographies for others. People can come to you for writing requests, you can put yourself on the map by taking your passion and using it for something much bigger. Use it to become your own master.

Your passion is to help others? Start a teaching agency where you either physically help others to learn for example technology, or math or English. There are millions of people who do not know how to use technology. Or produce content of how to use technology, guidance and/or packages full of easy-to-use material. Use your passion to do something greater. It doesn't have to be something like this either, you can choose how you want to do it, because at the end of the day, it is all your choice and no one else′s. Use it to become your own master.

Your passion is to make wine glasses? You might have grown up in a family who´s been producing wine glasses for years and you see it as bigger business opportunity. Start a Shopify store, build a website and sell wine glasses online. If you see an opportunity, include customization of the glasses.
Use it to become your own master.

The opportunities you think about could be exactly what you need and could be the difference you have been looking for. You will never know unless you try. Rather try something than thinking about what it could have been. Just imagine Mark Zuckerberg thinking about Facebook but chose not to act. Or Elon Musk thinking about Tesla but chose not to act on it. Or Jeff Bezos. Bill gates. Steve Jobs. The list is endless. Want to create something greater? Try. Act on it. Unleash your inner beast.

Whatever your passion is, whatever you love doing, could be turned into a beneficial and profitable job or side hustle. I will come back to the importance of imagination later on, but for now, just imagine yourself, quitting a job you hate, to start a business based on your passion. How amazing could it be to wake up, head to a job you love and make a great living out of it. If you don't love something, you can´t do it 100% great, even though you may be a perfectionist. You can´t be great and be your personal best in a job that you hate, you just can´t.

On the other hand, there is nothing holding you back from being amazing in something that you love. To top it off, you would not only be making a great living out of your passion, but you would also love every second of your time at work. Imagine this for a second, and write down your passions, and three ways to exploit your love for it in form of developing a business. For example, you love drawing, how can you make money of it? Another example, you love making illustrations in Adobe Illustrations, how can you make a living out of it?

When you think about it. Any hobby out there, either if it's running, cycling, football, fishing, or if it's a sport related to video games, golf or whatever it might be. Someone is making money out of it. Someone is making massive money out of what others love and share as their hobby. Millions of people like to read, tons of people make money from writing books and magazines.

"One person's hobby is another person's business."
- Hakon R Hagen

Under Armour was founded in 1996 by Kevin Plank. They manufacture footwear as well as sports and casual apparel. They are huge. 15,800 employees and revenues on $5.2 billion in 2018. The company was founded because when Kevin was playing football back in college. The T-shirt under his jersey always got sweat-soaked after every game and practice, but at the same time he noticed that the compression pants stayed dry. He figured that it could be the same for the T-shirts too. This is how it all started, and it has turned out to be an amazing story. People's hobbies is his business. He earns money on people enjoying sports and getting sweaty.

His passion was sports, football in particular, but to say it mildly, he turned it into profits. This is obviously not a story for everyone starting a business, but it's a sign of possibilities. Possibilities of success. Of hope and of something much bigger.

Create Jobs For Others

"I find that the harder I work, the more luck I seem to have"

- *Thomas Jefferson*

By starting for yourself, you will in many cases need employees to assist you on your journey to growth and success. Assuming that growth is what you dream of. Be aware, my friends, growth is not always beneficial and a good thing. With growth comes many factors along, but more about this in the next chapter.

When a business is founded, not only are tons of new possibilities available for you, but also some of the millions of people available in the labor market. By hiring fitting employees, you might take the business to new heights and a good work environment would be established.

You will have the possibility to hire people, train them and shape them to perfectly fit your company, purpose and strategies. Imagine that. You used to work for someone else, but now you started for yourself and you are hiring and training your own employees.

In addition to imagining that, imagine also the feeling, the proud feeling of accomplishment and the feeling of creating something greater. Something you have been meant to do for a long time. And finally, the steps have been taken and the decisions have been made. You. Are. Now. Your. Own. Boss.

"

I

Am

My

Own

Boss

"

Growth Might Be Good, But It Might Also Be Death

"Don't be afraid to give up the good to go for the great"
-   John D. Rockefeller

Small is the new big when it comes to new businesses. Just think about it. You open up your own business, you work for yourself, you are the only one to pay, you work from home which saves you costs of renting a space and equipment, you work from your own computer, no need to commute etc. Quick side thought about keeping the business small while earning big. I just finished reading "Company of One" by Paul Jarvis. He really puts it into perspective of how beneficial it can be to keep the business small. I highly recommend reading his book, it gave me tons of inspiration and many new ideas. With new technology comes new opportunities. Not only for starting a business, but also for running it.

As the Shopify example, you have the costs of building a website for the business as well as monthly costs of $19 dollars for keeping the page running.

You can watch videos on YouTube on how to develop a Shopify drop shipping store with AliExpress. Learn it in and out in no time. It doesn't require any storage and has low startup costs, so it it´s a reasonable idea to begin with. You have a total of $39 dollars for Shopify and AliExpress. You sell products in the fitness clothing industry and you add a 50% on the retail price and you target a group willing to pay it. Obviously, the purchasing power of your customers will depend on the country you target. I recommend researching your potential market and evaluate thereafter.

To put it into perspective, you sell products for $100 000 dollars a year, from which you receive $50 000 into your own pockets because 50% is the percentage you chose to add onto your products as your share.

However, you have costs of $39 dollar per months which equals $468 dollars a year in costs. The beauty of this is that as soon as the drop shipping store is established, the only thing you have to do is to accept orders and send products. It couldn´t be less work related to it and it could give you $49 532 dollars a year through this one online business. Build five of them and you got yourself $250k a year. Theoretically of course. Although, this is also excluding potential marketing costs, taxes, insurance, potential registration costs etc. But do not panic, these costs won´t make a big dent in your earnings, just consider them more of a scratch.

However, this example is just theoretical, but very possible. It all depends on which products or services you choose to sell, which country you target, your prices and your added profits, as well as how you market your products. When it comes to marketing, I will come back to this in the next chapter with some tips and ideas.

On the other hand, if you want to take this business to new heights by growing it and scaling up the processes, more costs will follow. Increased labor costs, rental and equipment costs, computers, leases, paid lunch and vacations and so on. Although you grow the business to $1 million dollar in sales a year rather than $100 000, you might be left with the same income due to all the extra costs, but with a hell of a lot more stress and effort.

But of course, I will not hide the fact that massive organizations which are properly run, are usually also making more money than smaller businesses. But on the individual level, I believe the difference of income is not massive. But for now, think about your next steps, is it important for your business to grow?

Do the math, put it in numbers and run it multiple times to make sure you are correct. You wouldn't want to end up losing a profitable business just to have more employees, right?

How Can I Make Customers Find Me?

"Opportunities don't happen. You create them."

-    Chris Grosser

When it comes to marketing, there are tons of good options to choose from, whereof all of them have different costs and proven effects related to them. Online advertisement such as Google Ads is a great place to start, however it is a costlier way to market than for example Instagram marketing or Facebook ads. The reach on both of them are absolute massive. There is no one you cannot reach if you want to reach them.

I will not go into detail of how to set up an ad on the different platforms or the costs related to them, you´ll find amazing and detailed guides on YouTube, Google and even social media platforms for it.

However, I will let you in on my personal favorites; Be aware, it all depends on your target group, what you´re focusing on and your budget. If you are targeting the older generation, Instagram advertisement might not be the best idea. Here are my three favorites:

- Facebook ads
- Google ads
- Email marketing

The thing with email marketing is that it might take some time to build up a sufficient email list. However, don't be afraid, there are tons of detailed guides of how you can make this happen in no time. Just google "How can I build up an email marketing list".

I prefer Facebook ads for their massive reach and relatively low prices compared to Google ads. You can easily reach thousands of people within a few days, but then again, it all depends on how good these leads are. Because in the end, how much is an unconverted lead worth? Over time they might come back due to the aftereffects of the ad. However, this is difficult to measure, and I recommend focusing on the direct leads which are measurable.

Google ads is a little more expensive than the other ways of marketing, but there is a reason why Google ads are as famous as they are. I mean, they can be so accurate and hit the perfect fitting client in no time when they Google the keywords of your choice. Google also provides an amazing overview of how the ad is performing, who is clicking it, demographics, locations etc.

The best part is that after having an ad live, you can use these detailed overviews to specify the next ad and to narrow it down to increase the probability of hitting the perfect lead.

This will increase conversion rate, reach more clients for less money.

To put this into perspective, according to Google themselves, there are around 5.6 billion searches on Google every single day. That's some serious potential right there.

Take advantage of these massive opportunities, but don't necessarily take the first option you look into. Check out multiple advertisement methods, see the costs, cost per click etc., see the potential reach and read about the methods and the success of others before you. Reviews of products and services are there to be read.

Imagination and Goals

"Opportunities don't happen. You create them"

- Henry David Thoreau

In this book there are two elements which have the power of changing your whole life, your whole business and future, and can be the difference between being an employee and an employer.

I have been talking about the power of imagination previously in this book, and the power of imagination is not the be messed with, nor is it to be joked about. If you imagine yourself owning a business building in the middle of LA with your name all over the door, you can do it. But you can't just lay in bed and think how nice it would be. You got to imagine how awesome it would be, how you can do it, how you can get there, what you have to do to get there. Channel all your power into this imagination and this project.

Constantly imagine it and constantly compare it to your current situation. By comparing what you could have, to what you have, it might trigger your inner strength and help you make that choice of starting a new life. Not just a new life, a brand-new journey is about to be entered. Not only entered either, it's about to be taken over, occupied and owned by you. We both know that if you set full sails towards a massive goal, you got to own it. You can't just borrow it on a Saturday afternoon when you feel good, but you got to own it every day of the week. It's yours and no one can take it away from you! Imagine exactly what you desire and want. Ask yourself how you can achieve it. How you can get it and how fast. Don't whisper it inside you, say it out loud, write it down and carry it with you.

Write down your reasons why you want to achieve these exact things and if you are feeling down, look at your reasons why, use it to get back on your feet and get the sails back up. If you prefer car metaphors, put it in sixth gear and throw the mirrors out, so you can't ever look back.

One thing is to imagine it, but another this is to have a goal of having it like this. Goals are full of power and it bring massive motivation with it. It can also bring structure, dedication and time management which we will discuss further later on.

But a goal is not just a goal. You have to have long term goals and short-term goals, they have to be clear, measurable and realistic. Sure, they can be as ambitious as you want, but the best goals are always realistic goals. Write them down, keep them with you and be proud of them. Print them out in massive sizes, frame them and hang them up on your walls at home and where you spend most of your time. Feel its power and own them. Always be reminded of your goals and have them in your focus at all times. Dedicate time, power and energy into your goals and you will succeed, it's just a matter of time.

I want you to tell yourself about your goals every morning when you wake up and every night before you go to bed. Channel your energy to these exact purposes. Additionally, while eating breakfast, write down your goals for the day and for the week. What do you want to accomplish, how many clients do you want to work with today or how many sales do you want to make?

Goals for today	Goals for this week

Draw up a drawing like the one above, or one of your own preferences and include your daily goals as well as your weekly goals. These are separate from your short-term goals in my definition, because the short-term goals are up to three to six months. For example, "in three months I want to have 100 new clients" or "in six months I want to have $100 000 in sales".

Your imagination is as powerful as you make it and your only limit is yourself. You can decide how far you can get, and as long as you have faith, positivity as well as clear and realistic goals, there is nothing you can't accomplish.

A game changing tips for me, early on, was to say three positive thing every morning. I was struggling with too much negativity for a period of time until I read a book. It turned me upside down. I became a new man. The book taught me many things, but the positivity is something that instantly helped me and has stuck with me ever since. **Try it, and you will never be the same again.**

The book was a mentality book written by an ex-special force soldier. I would highly recommend reading a similar book which focuses on mental strength and how to use the mind to your advantage. It could help you see things in a new and better way. Things you usually looked at negatively, might become a new opportunity.

No matter which book you read on topics related to business, they will all tell you the same. Goals are an absolute necessity if you want to achieve something greater than what you are having today.

I mean, think about it, and yes, I agree, I am telling you to think about many things, but if you don't do it, who will? No one will think about anything for you and tell you what you need to hear, you have to realize these things yourself. I am happy to say that since you are reading this book, I assume you are aware of this fact.

However, back to business. Think about how goals work. You set a goal, you want to accomplish your best and achieve your them. Over time, you manage to achieve them, and you feel so damn great. You set bigger goals and bigger goals. Suddenly, you have built up such a confidence to write down "I want to have my own business". You write this down and you will never be the same. Because soon, you will have your own business and your boss, is you.

You grow and suddenly write down "I want to have $ 1 million in sales this year". Two years later you aim to earn $10 million and more and more and more over time. Again, the only limit is you, and you can decide your own future. How much do you want to earn or what do you want to accomplish?

Fill out the empty lines below and fill in the first thoughts which comes to mind, and the first number that hits your head.

This is a common practice to map out your thoughts and motivation. To see for yourself, in words, what you want and what you desire.

Today I want to _____
This week I want to _____
This month I want to _____
This half year I want to _____
This year I want to _____

Today I want to earn_____
This week I want to earn _____
This month I want to earn_____
This half year I want to earn _____
This year I want to earn_____

The first five lines are focusing on what you want to accomplish in form of unmaterialistic goals, while the last five lines are pure materialistic related goals. What do you want to earn?

No matter what you put down above, you are underestimating yourself. You can do better and you know it, but always put down ambitious and massive goals. This makes it all more challenging and interesting. That's the fascinating part about goals. You think they might be too high, but you will be surprised of what you are actually capable of doing when you put your mind on it and dedicate your time to it.

It really is hard to put into words how important it is to take advantage of the power of goals and imagination. Clear goals. Massive imagination.

Two elements which can move mountains if used correctly. In addition to write down your goals, I want you to imagine your future every day, either in the morning or before bed. Even better, do it a couple of times a day.

Just lay down, close your eyes and imagine how you want your future to turn out. It can consist of anything you want, if it is a massive house next to a lake with ten cars in the garage, or if it is to have a business pulling in hundreds of millions in revenue a year. The bigger the better because the bigger the imagination is, the more you want it. The more you want it, the more you will be willing to work for it. This is key.

The more you are willing to work and dedicate your time to, the bigger things you are able to build and accomplish. This philosophy has created tons of millionaires and billionaires over the period of time they have existed, because I mean, no successful businessperson is lazy, uninspired and unmotivated.

There is a massive power behind every driven successful person. Something from either within or from the outside is driving them. Making them thrive and keep pushing. It might be internal, it might be external, but regardless of the motivation, they have it, and so do you. Find your driver, find your internal or external power source.

Establish a Road Map

"The way to get started is to quit talking and begin doing."

-     Walt Disney

Throughout the book we have used the term "key" many times regarding multiple elements which is a necessity within business, but this chapter "Establishing a road map", is the real key. This is a key, that is not only unlocking a door full of possibilities, but the whole damn gate.

A clearly established road map will constantly guide you towards your goals. Having a road map gives you clarity and is a necessity for knowing what to do in upcoming situations.

To put it in perspective, have you ever walked in an unknown forest without a map or a guiding tool? Either you will get lost, or luckily find your way out, or most likely you will walk around for hours and hours until your out of energy and motivation. This can be compared with starting a business without a clearly established road map. Without it, you might succeed, you might get lost, but you will probably end up being unsecure of where to go next and what to do.

A road map is your strategy, your way forward, which goals and which milestones do you want to achieve next?

When will you reach your definition of success? The road map also includes your vision for the business, your mission and the reason behind the business. This is a big part of the establishment process in the beginning of the business, and definitely a necessary one.

This will help you and your potential employees to work towards the same goals at all times and keep everyone on the same highway. Keep the goals, milestones and employees in the same car. But make sure it's clearly defined to avoid any type of confusion and misunderstandings later on. Communication is an absolute necessity. Be clear on messages between employees or customers.

Confusion is much scarier than it sounds and could mean some seriously bad news over time but could also be handled and cleared out of the way in no time. For what it's worth, avoid confusion to your greatest extent because confusion could be like a rolling snowball in a steep hill. It collects more trouble the further it rolls.

What Is Holding You Back?

"The real test is not whether you avoid this failure, because you won't. It's whether you let it harden or shame you into inaction, or whether you learn from it; whether you choose to persevere."

- Barack Obama

Why haven't you taken the step into the world filled with options and opportunities that are only controlled by you, and perhaps money, fame or success? I am sure there are many reasons why you haven't done it yet, but there are no actually legit reasons why you can't or shouldn't do it now.

There will never be a perfect time to take the leap with a bullet-proof plan with a guarantee of providing you and your family with tons of money or anything like that. But there are potential for it, massive potential if pursued with belief, faith, dedication and hard work. Compared to if you keep working for others and making others rich, there is no hope or potential for success.

So, really, what is actually holding you back? Why haven't you taken the step into the world of possibilities? Why haven't you entered one of the many doors offering a new life filled with possibilities. Doors with your name on it. A business you represent, you control and where you have the final say.

Let's reverse back to the beautiful time of imagination. One of the main tools on your journey to something bigger. When I say journey, I don't mean a slow path in an old Volvo, I mean the highway in a shiny electric car because that is where the world is headed. Because in this world it's either the highway, or no-way, and since you are reading this book, I have a feeling that you are not looking to take the no-way, simply because you want to jump right onto the highway. And that, my friend, is the correct decision.

I haven't pursued my dream because	What I will do to pursue my dream from now on
Timing hasn't been right? Not sure how? Don't have the resources?	

Now I want you to pick up a piece of paper and a pencil and draw a similar drawing as the one above. Fill it out with the truth and nothing but the truth, no lies, not even the white lies, and fill it out properly.

The thing with lies is that you are only tricking yourself, you're not tricking anyone else. So, fill out the drawing with the pure truth and give yourself a chance to see why you haven't pursued your dream yet, and be honest with yourself.

Make a Decision and Stick To It

"There are no secrets to success. It is the result of preparation, hard work, and learning from failure."

-     Colin Powell

Make a decision, any decision, and stick with it. Don´t spend time or energy second guessing your decision, because whatever is done, is done. You decided on starting a business, it´s done. Stick with it, do the work, be dedicated and never look back.

Don´t bother making a decision of not starting your own business or to pursue the greater good for yourself and your family. That is not the topic of this book, neither should it be a topic for you.

If you decide on starting a business, decisions will come on a rolling band like one of those in a mass production factory. They will roll in and you got to knock each of them way out of the park and don´t look for them after clearing them out. When the decision is made it is final. This is key, my friend. Just think about it. If you would make a decision, two days later you will question it, another day later you will question it even more and it goes on until the point where you can´t stop thinking about it. This will result in either a panic attack or something along the lines of a burnout and guaranteed waste of time which should have been spent on handling clients.

That's why my rule is; a made decision is a final decision. End of story. I use this rule no matter the topic or discussion. This saves me a ton of energy and time which could have gone to second guessing a made decision.

After defining the multiple areas of why you should start something for yourself, what you can get out of it and the unlimited amounts of possibilities, we will look deeper into the WHY'S. The WHY is the whole reason behind any decision. A decision is made for a reason which is based on a why. That sentence might be chaotic but think about it for a second, it actually makes total sense.

What Is Your Why?

"In order to succeed, your desire for success should be greater than your fear of failure."

- Bill Cosby

Have you ever thought about why you do what you do and why you did what you did? Why are things like they are in general? Why did we end up in a world with massive CO_2 pollution resulting in global warming and why do we make the choices we do? Is it coincidental, is a greater purpose behind it or what is it? These are topics which can drive you nuts, so for our own sakes, let's avoid these questions and rather focus on questions like this:

1. Why do you want to start for yourself?
2. What is your passion?
3. What do you want to do with your life?
4. Why would you want an own business?
5. What drives you and what makes your heart go nuts in a potential business-related way?

These are all highly relevant questions and topics which must be answered to make a proper decision. In the end, it is difficult to say that a decision was wrongly made. I mean, would you know the outcome of a situation if you did it differently than what you did? Hypothetically: If you would have said "Yes" rather than "No" in a certain situation, what would have happened?

Write down all your WHY'S, no matter the size and put them together on a piece of paper. Look at them, read them out loud, think about them and figure out what drives you. Put together a compelling WHY which will last in the long run. In the ups and downs, what will keep you moving? Is it money? Is it being your own boss or is it the name on the wall? No matter the reason, as long as it drives you and make you perform on your top level, it doesn't matter. Money? Sure, that's a super legit WHY.

Everyone wants money, someone wants it more than others but that's up to you to decide, and the cool part is that no one can tell you what to think or do. It's up to you and your inner beast. Feed it with what it wants.

What feeds your beast? Is it a money beast or is it a name-on-the-wall-beast? Figure it out and use it for all its powers! Because as soon as you start, when you have decided to do something greater and work your ass off for it, there is no return. There is no way back, only up, and it sure is bright up there.

Be Realistic. Always.

"I never dreamed about success, I worked for it."

- Estee Lauder

Dreaming and imagination is key and extremely valuable. But always keep in mind that you got to be realistic about it and the work that follows. The bigger your dreams are, the more work is automatically attached to it.

What is more difficult: build a company with 10 employees or 1000 employees? It´s relatively obvious, correct?

I love to daydream about what I want in the future, how my house will look like, what I want to accomplish etc. Personally, I try not to be too materialistic because having a bunch of cars in my garage is not what motivates me. However, if that is what motivates you, then go for it. Dream of having a thousand cars in there! Imagine how hard you will work for it if that is you biggest dream.

The point of this chapter is actually just to remind you that no matter what you want in life, you got to work for it, and the bigger dreams you have, the more work is required.

No one has become a millionaire by watching Netflix. Everything requires action, it´s just up to you, and you only, to decide what your next step will be. Will it be real action, or will it be an action movie on Netflix?

No matter what the choice is or will be, you are the one with all the power. You are the one who decides what the next step will be. That's the great part, you can decide whatever you like and the only responsible one is. Ultimately, it teaches you a lesson that you can't learn anywhere else.
No book can teach you how to make a decision and no guide can show you what to do in your specific situation. They will help you on your journey, they will inspire and motivate you, but they won't directly show you what to do. Take the knowledge and motivation it provides, and "learn by doing". Go for it!

Got Knocked Down? Then Get The H***
Back Up!

"The successful warrior is the average man, with laser-like focus."

- Bruce Lee

This chapter requires more than just one quote. I use quotes all the time, because I mean, who doesn't like a great quote? Getting knocked down, experiencing failure or a loss is all part of business. And these are all business-related contexts of course. What can you do when something negative happens? Either in form of failure, the idea didn't work out or you run out of resources to carry your business, sit down for a sec. Think about it and get back into it. Shake off all the bad and negative thoughts and figure out your next move. Because there's always a next move.

"Would you like me to give you a formula for success? It's quite simple, really: Double your rate of failure. You are thinking of failure as the enemy of success. But it isn't at all. You can be discouraged by failure or you can learn from it, so go ahead and make mistakes. Make all you can. Because remember that's where you will find success."

- Thomas J. Watson

It's quite crazy, right? Successful people with tons of experience and great tips in their back pocket, are basically telling you to fail more. This sounds a little ironic, correct? Well, failure teaches you valuable lessons you can't learn anywhere else, and what made you fail one time, will never hit you again. There are certain things which has to be experienced in person and can't be taught through a book or another source.

Except of the feeling of failure or success, most of the things you need to know about business, either how to succeed or how to start a business, are easily accessible on free tools online. The only thing it takes is time, dedicated and self-discipline.

"If you really want to do something, you'll find a way. If you don't, you'll find an excuse."

-    Jim Rohn

Define Your Own Success

"Success is walking from failure to failure with no loss of enthusiasm."

- Winston Churchill

As mentioned previously in this book, there are various types of rich and everyone has their own definition of success. How do you know if you have succeeded if you don't know what success is to you? Is it having an income of $100 000 a year? Is it having a passive income of $5000 a month through either an online business, an ad service or whatever it might be? You have to have a clear definition of what you consider as a success. This is the only way to live up to your goals and to tell yourself that you have succeeded and that you won.

Without defining it, you cannot write "this year I want to succeed with my own business". Because by at end of the year, when you would look back to check if you were successful, you might be confused and think "but what was actually my success this year"? Let's skip this confusion and define the term "success" immediately

Yet again, grab a piece of paper and your favorite pen, and write down clearly what success is to you. You don't have to draw a similar drawing as the one below this time, you can be creative and draw up your own idea. I mean, in the end, the drawing below is just a straight line.

For me, success is:
<u> </u>

- To have my own online business with $100 000 in sales in 2020
- I want to get 100 new clients
- I want to purchase an apartment

Not only define the term, but also write down a plan of how you can accomplish these successes. For example, I want to get 60 of those new clients through Google ads, 30 of them through Facebook ads and the rest through "word of mouth" and through organic search.

I will charge each client an X amount on average to call the year 2020 a success. Whatever it might be for you, it is extremely valuable to you to get a clear view of what success for you actually is. This will help your inner beast to work harder, to achieve more, and to achieve what you decided to set as a goal.

When getting a customer, give them the best service you possibly can. Over time, this can be worth more than any marketing method out there. Just imagine, when you are the customer and you are extremely satisfied with a purchase, do you brag about it to friends and family? Damn right you do. You brag it up in the skies.

This is the word of mouth, and it is damn powerful. A happy customer can lead you to tens of more sales over time later on. The customer is always priority number one.

And be aware, this can also backlash if treated opposite. A dissatisfied customer can ruin your business. Of course, depending on your size, resources, location etc. But by all means, avoid a dissatisfied customer because is really can mess things up.

However, if it were to happen. Go the extra mile to make them happy again. Offer them something and have a proper follow up, show them that you care, this could avoid further "damage" and could repair certain damages which could already have been made.

The Power of Time Management

"All progress takes place outside the comfort zone."

\-   Michael John Bobak

Throughout this book we have mentioned multiple tools such as drawing simple tables to clearly write down goals. Use online tools such as Google, YouTube, Udemy and social media platforms for all they are worth. Spend time on these amazing free tools and collect all the knowledge you can.

Use imagination to the unlimited extent. Imagine whatever you want and work step by step towards it, because there are no overnight successes. As well as other tools we have gone through, I want to introduce one more.

Proper time management can give you tons of extra time. It doesn't physically give you more hours in a day, obviously, but by controlling your time you will be able to get more things done, and that even in a shorter period of time. Your effectivity will fly through the roof and it will be an absolute game changer. It will literally change the whole game.

Imagine handling 10 clients in one day rather than five clients. That's an 100% increase just by managing your time. However, how to manage this is up to each individual, which tools they use etc. You can use a visual online board like

Trello or Asana, these are great ones. They allow you to visually write down tasks, project plans, timelines and they are both worth checking out.

At the same time, you can stick to old school methods such as using one of those big white physical board and a big pencil. Write down what you want to do and when.

These tools are amazing for short-term purposes, but for a long-term goal, a timeline could be a superb choice. An example below is a yearlong timeline. You can do it for as long as you want to. Put in specific milestones, how you can achieve them and by when. What happens if you reach these milestones? What happens if you don't reach them?

Jan 2020  Dec 2020

The timeline is just an example and can also be used for short-term purposes. Even as short as a day can be fitted into one of these.

For example: Go for a run at 7am. Shower and eat before 8.30am. Handle client one by 9am. Send out email by 9.30am. Call client two at 9.40am. You get the point. Keep putting down your timelines, but don't make it too crazy. Give yourself some buffer, some room to breathe, to eat and drink, and to refresh. I mean, after all, what good is a powerful engine without any oil? This will help you manage your time and focus on your main priorities. It will also help you avoid spending time on unnecessary activities and time-consuming waste.

Pride

"Never give in except to convictions of honor and good sense."

- Winston Churchill

We have talked about finding your WHY'S, your desires, your definitions of rich and what you feed your beast to keep grinding. We also went through the power of imagination. So, let's reverse back, let's talk about imagination, one more time.

Let's imagine that you start your own business after working your whole life for someone else's benefit. You sold your time, and your soul, every day from 9am-5pm for a fixed salary. But not anymore. Now, you have your own business, and you chose to rent an office space because your business requires employees and more space.

On the building, your name is branded all over it. In capital letters your name hangs on a tall building in a congested area. Thousands and thousands of people drive by it every day looking at it and wishing it was theirs. People who drive by wonder who the name belongs to.

They google it, they search in the local newspaper, they check their social media, and they find you. Suddenly, thousands of people find your name, your face, and you're suddenly a well-known person in the community. A community consisting of thousands of people who now respect you, know who you are and greet you on the streets.

You have made it. You made a decision of achieving something greater. Not necessarily for money, not for the fame or for the greeting on the street, but for the feeling of pride. It's yours, your name on the wall and your business. People come to you for help, for tips and for guidance.

You're like a book being placed on the top shelf being sold for the highest price, like the biggest shark in the ocean. Not with a purpose to do anything with your power, but have a feeling of respect, pride and opportunities.

How would you feel about having something like this and being someone like this? Being this person in the streets that other people say hi to, who respect you. This might not be your dream scenario, but it is an example of what could be yours. Imagine your own scenario, write it down and read it over and over again. Imagine how it makes you feel, how proud you would be, which thoughts would run through your head. Make them detailed. Make them real.

Keep Grinding

"There is a powerful driving force inside every human being that, once unleashed, can make any vision, dream, or desire a reality."

- Tony Robbins

Consistency in your road to something bigger and constant work based on inspiration, belief and motivation. This is the formula to a greater purpose with your own business with your name branded all over it. It´s not enough with Monday – Thursday motivation and the rest of the week off. Keep grinding for something bigger.

Keep working for your dream and bigger purpose for your life. We both know you can do it and you´re already on the highway. Make sure you´re not driving off onto a smaller, congested side street where you slow down and will get stuck in traffic. Stick to the highway because that´s where the big things are happening. This is where the lane is clear, and the big guys are driving.

Do you think business owners drive off onto a smaller side street every Friday – Sunday to relax? Never. They stick to the highway. Always. Do you think successful people go home from work on Thursday and wait all the way until Monday to start grinding again? Never.

Want to be successful? Stick to the highway and don't you ever turn off. Want to reach your massive goals of having tons of money, fame, time with your family or whatever your definition of success is? Work on your dream, establish it, grow it, pay attention to it and be proud of it.

Since you are reading this book, you are already on the path to something much bigger. Something greater which will change your life. It won't be this book changing your mind or telling your inner beast to go nuts. It's already awaken and ready to work, ready to grind and ready to make a proper change. But, are you ready to release it?

Recommended resources

"A successful man is one who can lay a firm foundation with the bricks that other throw at him."

- David Brinkley

This chapter is dedicated to offer you some resources which I would personally recommend. I do this, because these resources have added a lot of value to me, in form of either inspiration, knowledge or motivation. They fed me like a proper Christmas dinner. They each added their own value, which together build something bigger inside me.

Books

- Money – Master the game - Tony robbins
- Rich Dad, Poor Dad – Robert Kiyosaki
- The 4-Hour Work Week – Timothy Ferriss
- $100 Startup – Chris Guillebeau
- The Six Figure Second Income – Daniel Kahneman
- 10X Rule – Grant Cardone
- The 7 Habits of Highly Effective People – Stephen Covey
- The Intelligent Investor – Benjamin Graham
- Principles – Ray Dalio

- Thing & Grow Rich – Napoleon Hill
- The Lean Startup – Eric Ries

People

- Tony Robbins
- Grant Cardone
- Elon Musk
- Jeff Bezos
- Bill Gates
- Oprah Winfrey
- Michelle Obama
- Beyonce

These are all famous people. Along with many others, they offer tons of great inspiration and knowledge. But I would also like to forward some attention to upcoming inspirators with massive challenges ahead.

- Greta Thunberg – Environmentalist
- Boyan Slat – The Ocean Cleanup
- Leonardo DiCaprio - Environmentalist
- Melinda Gates – Co-Founder of Bill & Melinda Foundation

Podcasts & Audibles

- The Tony Robbins Podcast
- The Tim Ferriss Show
- Startup Podcast
- Entrepreneurs on Fire
- RISE AND GRIND
- How to get and stay motivated – Grant Cardone
- Be Obsessed or Be Average – Grant Cardone

There are tons of books available on audibles these days, and there are continuously flowing in new ones. I love audibles. They're great. Grab your headphones and listen to pure knowledge either while walking, while working out or while laying on bed. Let the inspiration flow into your ears. Let it motivate you.

Mentor

Additionally, having someone who can assist you, give you guidance and support on your journey can be of huge help. No matter what your journey is, it can be extremely helpful to have someone as a mentor. Not everyone fits to be someone's mentor. It is a very individual choice and can only be made by you. However, to get on the right path, it could also be beneficial to take advantage of coaching.

www.ingramcontent.com/pod-product-compliance
Lightning Source LLC
Chambersburg PA
CBHW020601220526
45463CB00006B/2406